THE GAME MAKER'S LEVEL DESIGN SKETCHBOOK

Name: _____
Date: _____

away with the pixels
awaywiththepixels.com

Notes

LEVEL: _____

NOTES:

LEVEL: _____

NOTES:

LEVEL: _____

NOTES:

LEVEL: _____

NOTES:

LEVEL: _____

NOTES:

LEVEL: _____

NOTES:

LEVEL: _____

NOTES:

LEVEL: _____

NOTES:

LEVEL: _____

NOTES:

LEVEL: _____

NOTES:

LEVEL: _____

NOTES:

LEVEL: _____

NOTES:

LEVEL: _____

NOTES:

LEVEL: _____

NOTES:

LEVEL: _____

NOTES:

LEVEL: _____

NOTES:

LEVEL: _____

NOTES:

LEVEL: _____

NOTES:

LEVEL: _____

NOTES:

LEVEL: _____

NOTES:

LEVEL: _____

NOTES:

LEVEL: _____

NOTES:

LEVEL: _____

NOTES:

LEVEL: _____

NOTES:

LEVEL: _____

NOTES:

LEVEL: _____

NOTES:

LEVEL: _____

NOTES:

LEVEL: _____

NOTES:

LEVEL: _____

NOTES:

LEVEL: _____

NOTES:

LEVEL: _____

NOTES:

LEVEL: _____

NOTES:

LEVEL: _____

NOTES:

LEVEL: _____

NOTES:

LEVEL: _____

NOTES:

LEVEL: _____

NOTES:

LEVEL: _____

NOTES:

LEVEL: _____

NOTES:

LEVEL: _____

NOTES:

LEVEL: _____

NOTES:

LEVEL: _____

NOTES:

LEVEL: _____

NOTES:

LEVEL: _____

NOTES:

LEVEL: _____

NOTES:

LEVEL: _____

NOTES:

LEVEL: _____

NOTES:

LEVEL: _____

NOTES:

LEVEL: _____

NOTES:

LEVEL: _____

NOTES:

LEVEL: _____

NOTES:

LEVEL: _____

NOTES:

LEVEL: _____

NOTES:

LEVEL: _____

NOTES:

LEVEL: _____

NOTES:

LEVEL: _____

NOTES:

LEVEL: _____

NOTES:

LEVEL: _____

NOTES:

LEVEL: _____

NOTES:

LEVEL: _____

NOTES:

LEVEL: _____

NOTES:

LEVEL: _____

NOTES:

LEVEL: _____

NOTES:

LEVEL: _____

NOTES:

LEVEL: _____

NOTES:

LEVEL: _____

NOTES:

LEVEL: _____

NOTES:

LEVEL: _____

NOTES:

LEVEL: _____

NOTES:

LEVEL: _____

NOTES:

LEVEL: _____

NOTES:

LEVEL: _____

NOTES:

LEVEL: _____

NOTES:

LEVEL: _____

NOTES:

LEVEL: _____

NOTES:

LEVEL: _____

NOTES:

LEVEL: _____

NOTES:

LEVEL: _____

NOTES:

LEVEL: _____

NOTES:

LEVEL: _____

NOTES:

LEVEL: _____

NOTES:

LEVEL: _____

NOTES:

LEVEL: _____

NOTES:

LEVEL: _____

NOTES:

LEVEL: _____

NOTES:

LEVEL: _____

NOTES:

LEVEL: _____

NOTES:

LEVEL: _____

NOTES:

LEVEL: _____

NOTES:

LEVEL: _____

NOTES:

LEVEL: _____

NOTES:

LEVEL: _____

NOTES:

LEVEL: _____

NOTES:

LEVEL: _____

NOTES:

LEVEL: _____

NOTES:

LEVEL: _____

NOTES:

LEVEL: _____

NOTES:

LEVEL: _____

NOTES:

LEVEL: _____

NOTES:

LEVEL: _____

NOTES:

LEVEL: _____

NOTES:

Made in United States
North Haven, CT
19 December 2024